Tana
Hoban

All About Where

Greenwillow Books, New York

6414

The full-color photographs were reproduced from 35-mm slides.
Greenwillow Books, a division of William Morrow & Company, Inc.,
105 Madison Avenue, New York, NY 10016.
Printed in Singapore by Tien Wah Press
First Edition   10 9 8 7 6 5 4 3 2 1

Library of Congress Cataloging-in-Publication Data
Hoban, Tana.
All about where / by Tana Hoban.
p.   cm.
Summary: Photographs illustrate location words
such as above, between, in, under, and behind.
ISBN 0-688-09697-2   ISBN 0-688-09698-0 (lib. bdg.)
1. English language—Prepositions—Juvenile literature.
[1. English language—Prepositions.]   I. Title.
PE1335.H6   1991   428.2—dc20
90-30849   CIP   AC

For all the children
everywhere

above
on
behind
under
out
against
across
between
in
through
beside
among
below
over
around

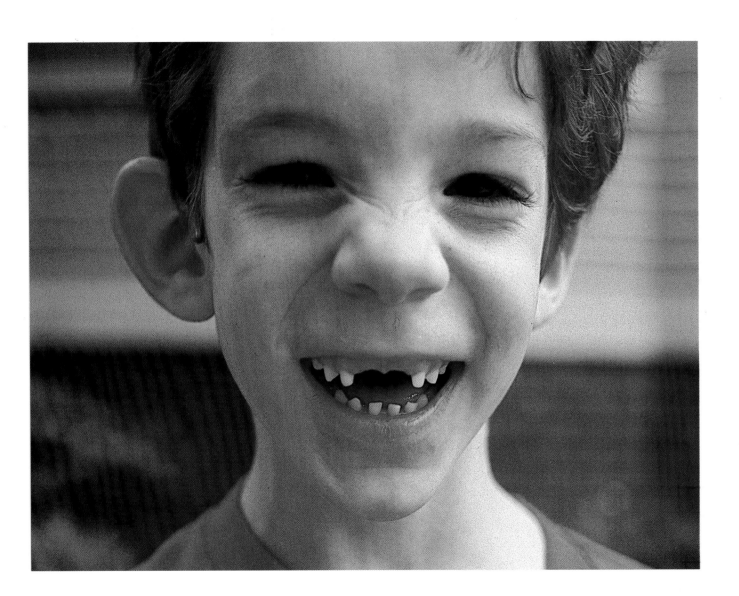

above

on

behind

under

out

against

across

between

in

through

beside

among

below

over

around

TANA HOBAN's photographs have
been exhibited at the Museum of
Modern Art in New York City and in
galleries around the world. She has
won many gold medals and prizes
for her work as a photographer and
filmmaker. Her books for children
are known and loved throughout
the world.